Copyright © 2024 Antionette Barnes All rights reserved

he characters and events portrayed in this book are fictitious.
Any similarity to real persons, living or dead,
is coincidental and not intended by the author.

No part of this book may be reproduced,
or stored in a retrieval system, or transmitted
in any form or by any means, electronic,
mechanical, photocopying, recording,
or otherwise, without express
written permission of the publisher.

ISBN: 978-1-7370589-3-9

Printed in the United States of America

Dedicated to my future, past, and even my present self.

Baby girl, we got this.

Keep motivating yourself.

Keep pushing forward.

-Poetic Tamara

Going Against Yourself

Late

"IS IT TOO LATE TO RECLAIM MY POWER?

WELL, TO FIND MY POWER PLEASE TELL ME IT'S NOT TOO LATE"

Going Against Yourself

By: Antionette Barnes

Table of contents:

1. Attention
2. Hug on me
3. Not your type
4. All in love
5. Who would have thought?
6. Focus shifted
7. Energy
8. Covered in tears
9. No guidance and support
10. Your image
11. Collided
12. Used to always bump heads
13. No outlet
14. Growth and maturity
15. Captured
16. Have an idea
17. Early in the mornings

18. Hug your dad
19. Withdraw
20. Full of
21. Split
22. Characters
23. Lead yourself
24. Stop
25. Describe
26. Simple
27. Came over me
28. I have confidence
29. When I was
30. Often
31. Clear
32. Declutter your mind
33. Direction
34. Force
35. Without
36. Silent

37. She loved herself enough to leave
38. Done missing you
39. Hold that thought
40. Be patient with yourself
41. Late
42. What are we doing?
43. Sinking quick
44. Only one who loves me
45. Individual
46. Against yourself
47. Go easy on yourself

Attention

I turned my focus on you
It was solely on you
I was so all about you
I let all the other ones go

Yeah, you had my attention
Now all that has changed
My attention got directed to somebody else
Somebody who is all about me

Now how does that make you feel
Knowing that you lost a real one?
You were so caught up in your ways
Thinking it was a privilege to talk to you

Well, yeah you lost my attention
My focus got shifted somewhere else
Now I'm all in love
Who would have thought that I would be in love?

"Knowing that you lost a real one?"

—*Poetic Tamara*

Poetic Tamara

Hug on me

Every time you come around me,
You have to touch me
All up on me
You always have to hug on me

Why do you always have to be physical with me?
Why can't we ever chill
Without all that touchy touchy?
You always have to hug on me

I'm the type of person
Who crave a different form of intimacy
Stimulate my mind
Without any form of physical contact

> "Who crave a different form of intimacy"
> —*Poetic Tamara*

Poetry Lovers

Not your type

It's okay
Just admit it
That I'm not your type
I already know it

I just want the words
To pass through your lips
Leading me on
By a thread

That's what you were doing
I already knew
That I was not your type
Making me your girlfriend

Then eventually your wife
Is something that is not on your mind
You wouldn't let me go
Until I let you go

"Leading me on"

-Poetic Tamara

"I must get back to me."

All in love

I have been wondering and wondering
How does it feel to be in love
I want to be all in love
With the one who is for me

I've never been in love before
Only in lust
I want to feel the feeling
Of being all in love

I want to fall in love
With love itself
All in love
So in love

"I've never been in love before"
—*Poetic Tamara*

"Be great."

Who would have thought?

Falling in love
Wasn't easy
That was my love life
Love in all the wrong places

5

I couldn't find the right place
Lust was all around me
Trying so hard
Not to fall for temptation

So, who would have thought
That love would have found me?
Who would have thought
Lust would have been replaced with love?

Who would have thought
That there is love for everybody?
Falling in love wasn't easy
Love came to me just at the right time

"Not to fall for temptation"

—Poetic Tamara

Write your own affirmation:

_____

_____

_____

_____

_____

6 Focus shifted

I started thinking about other stuff
Other stuff that would exercise my brain
My brain began opening to new ideas
That's what I called "focus shifted"

That old way of thinking
Didn't really matter to me
Ever since my focus shifted
I've been all about bettering myself

Focus shifted
Now living with a better way of thinking
Positive thinking
Positive vibes

> "Other stuff that would exercise my brain"
> —*Poetic Tamara*

"Focus on you"

There was way too much energy

That was wasted

Wasted on 'Energy Blvd.' where it should have said 'Energy Wasted Blvd.'

Energy that can't be given back

So, I took my single self

Down towards 'Falling In Love Blvd.'

Where I turned the corner onto 'Loving Yourself Blvd.'

Where I vowed to myself

That there will be no more energy wasted

Wasted on the wrong person

Then I took my single self

To 'Take It Slow Ave.'

Where I vowed to learn

The ways of the wise

To learn how to

Get to 'Get Hooked Ave.'

> Where I turned the corner onto 'Loving Yourself Blvd.'
>
> —*Poetic Tamara*

Write your own affirmation (s):

_____

_____

_____

_____

_____

Covered in tears

Yo,
So, check this out
I've been feeling alone
No, I've been feeling lonely lately

Do they mean the same thing?
Someone tell me
What I do know
Is that I've been covered in tears

Covered in tears
It started to feel like I was drowning
Looking for a hand to pull me up
Listening out for some comforting voices

These ears of mine
Didn't hear no voice of that sort
This face of mine
Was fully covered in tears

Covered in tears

My eyesight was blurry

These tears of mine kept flowing down

Flowing down for what seems to be a lifetime

"Is that I've been covered in tears"

—**Poetic Tamara**

Poetry Lovers

Jote down how you are feeling in the present moment

_____

_____

_____

_____

_____

_____

No guidance and support

What people don't know is
That I have been going through life
For what seems like by myself
From childhood to adulthood

I wasn't taught many stuff
I had no guidance and support
I have not been taught stuff by anyone
I have been keeping this to myself

No guidance and support
Really messed me up
Had me doing things
I shouldn't have been doing

Paths crossed with people
That shouldn't have been crossed
Those were paths
Where I was looking for love in

I just needed guidance and support
I needed to be guided down the right path
And supported while I was going down there
All the while, I had no guidance and support

"From childhood to adulthood"

—*Poetic Tamara*

Jote down how you are feeling in the present moment

_____

_____

_____

_____

_____

_____

Your image

10

It took me a while
But I finally realized
That I didn't fit your image
I wasn't even close

Your view of me
Was not your representation of yourself
I thought we had a connection
A connection that was good for your image

I was under the wrong impression
I wasn't good for your image
I wasn't the type of person who you wanted to show off
I finally know that you were protecting your image

"Was not your representation of yourself"
—Poetic Tamara

Poetic Tamara

Collided

Worlds collided
That wasn't supposed to meet
Shatter into pieces
Is what happened to their hearts

Collided
At the wrong time
Worlds fell apart
Between two people

Whose paths collided at the wrong time
Two lips meet
Two sets of arms wrapped around
The right one

But at the wrong time
Worlds collided
That wasn't supposed to meet
In this age of time

> "Shatter into pieces"
> —*Poetic Tamara*

Poetic Tamara

Used to always bump heads

12

If only there was a way
To make things better
Between you and I
So, then we wouldn't have bumped heads

You used to always make it hard
Hard to understand you
Hard to love you
That's why we used to always bump heads

Speaking my mind
Would have only made it worse at times
We used to always bump heads
Then turn around and make up later

I was looking for love
Within you
Wrong person,
Right idea

Or is it
Right person,
Right idea
And the wrong time?

Poetic Tamara

"Hard to understand you"

—Poetic Tamara

"There's poetry within all of us."

No outlet

For years and years
I had to keep things in
There were no outlets
I needed to pour my heart out

Walking around clueless
I seemed to be invisible to the world
I just needed that one outlet
I had too much on my heart

Or too much on my mind
I needed that one thing
To express myself to
Or just that one person

To hear me out
There were no outlet
Forced to keep things in
Forced to be left with my thoughts

"I needed to pour my heart out"

—Poetic Tamara

Write your own affirmation:

_____

_____

_____

_____

_____

_____

Growth and maturity

Thank God for growth and maturity
Old habits
Are dead in the past
The old me

Is dying from the inside
Going through a stage in my life called 'Growth'
Thank God for growth and maturity
Going through different stages in my life

Experiencing different emotions
All at once
I'm so truly at peace
I can feel the 'growth' within me

> Going through a stage in my life called 'Growth'
>
> —Poetic Tamara

Write your own affirmation:

_____

_____

_____

_____

_____

Captured

I captured your smile
Smiling bright with your white teeth
Your bottom lip looking juicy
Man, I love you

I captured us together
Real live happy moments
Those were the moments
That nothing in this world can steal my love from you

I captured you sleeping
All peaceful in our bed
Just for you to fade away
Then I woke up suddenly alone

"I captured us together"

—*Poetic Tamara*

poetry Lovers

Have an idea

You don't have to tell me you don't love me
I already sensed that
My intuition has been on high alert
I felt it

Your texts got short
Your responses became dry
It already came to me in a dream
More like a vision

I need to leave you alone3
That's the sign that I got
Leave you alone
Gone on by my business

I have an idea
Go on and be happy
Don't look back this way
I'm doing good

I have an idea
I'ma live my life
I found love within
I just want to be at peace

> "More like a vision"
> —*Poetic Tamara*

Write your own affirmation:

_____

_____

_____

_____

_____

rly in the mornings

ly in the mornings when I wake up
I turned on my back and lay still
    Eyes closed
    Body relaxed

I have to get myself ready for the morning
Doing a little meditation
while I'm lying there
Oh, how I love time to myself

Eyes closed
Body relaxed
Early in the mornings thinking of the day up ahead
Enjoying the quietness

> "Body relaxed"
> —Poetic Tamara

Write your own affirmation:

_____

_____

_____

_____

_____

Hug your dad

It might not be often
That you get this chance
So, while the chance is here
  Take advantage of it

  Hug your dad
  Love your dad
  Respect your dad
You might not always get this opportunity

  Hug your dad
  Spend time with your dad
  Make time to
  Bond with your dad

  Hug your dad
  Make sure to hug your dad
  Take the opportunity
  To show your dad some love

"Take the opportunity"
—Poetic Tamara

Jote down how you are feeling in the present moment

_____

_____

_____

_____

_____

_____

Withdraw

19

I used to do this a lot
Not knowing that it was unhealthy
This was back in my young days
Back in the days

Of no guidance and support
I didn't know how to communicate effectively
I didn't know how to express my emotions
So, I was afraid to express my emotions

Withdraw
I also went into withdrawal mode
I couldn't take how people spoke to me
I didn't how to respond

All I knew was to withdraw
Keep my thoughts to myself
Keep my emotions to myself
I had no outlet

So, bottled in is what happened
To my thoughts and emotions
I was operating out of a state of insecurity
And a state of low confidence

"I was operating out of a state of insecurity"

— *Poetic Tamara*

Jote down how you are feeling in the present moment

_____

_____

_____

_____

_____

Full of

Full of lies

Full of jealousy

Full of comparisons

This is not the way to live

Full of discouragement

Full of hate

Full of negativity

Get your life together

Full of love

Full of peace

Full of positivity

Live a life full of abundance

"Get your life together"

—Poetic Tamara

"Do it for you."

Split

I had to split from my old ways
The old ways
That was no longer serving me
I had to split

In order for me to become a better me
That separation from my old ways
Is one of the best things
That I have ever decided to do

I had decided
To make that split
While I was elevating my life
While I was going through my healing journey

"While I was elevating my life"
—Poetic Tamara

Write your own affirmation:

_____

_____

_____

_____

_____

_____

22 Characters

These characters in my life
Are not really inspirational
Well, there is only one
That one person is me

I'm the main character
In my life's story
I need more characters
In my life

New characters
Who comes with wisdom
Who are inspirational
I want characters

To be a part of my life
Who will stimulate my mind
And who will be meaningful to my life
These characters need to be replaced

"Who comes with wisdom"

—Poetic Tamara

"Be you. Be you. Be you."

Lead yourself

23

Get out of your way
I said what I said
You are blocking "You"
Don't you know that?

You're waiting for a leader
Look within you
Search within you
Find the leader who you seek

Within you
Be your own leader
Lead yourself
Trust yourself

Lead yourself down the right path
Lead yourself where you want to go
Lead yourself how you want to be lead
Be your own leader

"Lead yourself how you want to be lead"

—Poetic Tamara

Write your own affirmation:

_____

_____

_____

_____

_____

_____

Stop procrastinating
Stop blocking your own blessings
Move out of the way
You're in your own way

Stop playing around
Stop playing with your own emotions
Step out of the way
You have things to do with your life

I'm not playing with you
I mean what I said
Stop the negative thinking
Stop the doubting yourself

"Stop playing with your own emotions"

—Poetic Tamara

Note down how you are feeling in the present moment:

_____

_____

_____

_____

_____

Describe

Describe to me how you feel
Describe to me how you think your life is supposed to go
Describe to me how you think life is supposed to go
I'm here right now

Wanting to know
What's going on inside of your head
I'm checking up on your heart
I hope it's not hard for you to describe these things to me

Because I really want to know
Describe to me how you feel about me
Describe to me what you think about me
Look at me trying to make conversation with you

> "I'm checking up on your heart"
>
> —Poetic Tamara

Write your own affirmation:

_____

_____

_____

_____

_____

Simple

26

There are things that I wish were simple
I wish life was simple
I wish falling in love was simple
Why do things have to be hard?

Why can't things be simple?
As simple as me writing this?
Not simple conversations though
But simple communication

> "But simple communication"
> —Poetic Tamara

Note down how you are feeling in the present moment:

_____

_____

_____

_____

_____

_____

27 Came over me

I don't know what came over m[e]
I don't know what happened
Tears formed in my eyes
I wasn't thinking sad thoughts

My thoughts were focus
I didn't hold them back
I just let them flow down
What came over me?

Why was I experiencing that moment?
I thought to myself
That maybe I was having
An emotional detox

What came over me?
I had to speak to myself out loud
Let myself know that I was safe and secure
That I was on the right path and to trust the process

"Why was I experiencing that moment?"

—*Poetic Tamara*

Write your own affirmation (s):

_____

_____

_____

_____

_____

_____

28
I have confidence

I have confidence in myself
I have confidence in my abilities
I have confidence in my words
I found the power within

I have confidence in my walk
I have confidence in my affirmations
I have confidence in the way I dress
I have been gaining confidence

I have confidence in my body
I have confidence in my uniqueness
I have confidence in my willpower
I stand firm on that

> "I found the power within"
> —Poetic Tamara

Note down how you are feeling in the present moment:

___

___

___

___

___

When I was

When I was in a relationship,
    I felt alone
    I felt lonely
    I felt worthless

When I was going through my stages of being lonely,
I had nobody to turn to
Depression crept in and crept out a number of times
I used to get hit with loneliness hard

When I was re-evaluating my life,
It was hard for me to get right
When I did get right,
My mindset changed

When I was shifting my purpose
My mindset changed from that of a
'Fixed' mindset to that of a 'growth' mindset
I have been raising my vibration

"Depression crept in and crept out a number of times"

—*Poetic Tamara*

Poetry Lovers

Often

Often,
I sit by myself
Often,
I talk to myself

Often,
I go on walks by myself
Often,
I drive around by myself

Often,
I watch with my solo self
Often,
I read books with my solo self

"I sit by myself"
        —Poetic Tamara

"Make time to reflect."

Clear

31

I need clear messages
To the questions I ask
Clear and precise
I don't want to miss the message(s)

Assumptions
Will creep in
Not being heard
Will creep in

I will be all in my thoughts
Be clear with your words to me
Be clear with your intentions with me
So we can be on the same page

"I don't want to miss the message(s)"
— **Poetic Tamara**

"Reflect on what it is that you might need to reflect on

Declutter your mind

Free your mind of unwanted thoughts

Free your mind of negative thoughts

Make room in there

Declutter your mind

32

New information

Are waiting

To enter

Positive thoughts

Are on standby

For you to declutter your mind

Release!

Those thoughts are taking up space

Declutter your mind

Organize your thoughts

Spend time with yourself

Focus on what needs to be focused on

"Make room in there"
            —Poetic Tamara

Note down how you are feeling in the present moment:

_____

_____

_____

_____

_____

_____

Embrace being single

Don't do that to yourself
Questioning and questioning
Why this/why that?
Just let it be

33

For once in your life
You don't have to have all the answers
To all your questions
Slow your thinking

You're thinking too fast
I know you're still single
Relax!
It won't be for long

Take time out for yourself
It's a must
Focus, focus, focus
Embrace being single

"Take time out for yourself"

—Poetic Tamara

Write your own affirmation (s):

_____

_____

_____

_____

_____

_____

Teary

I have to quit doing this
I keep telling myself
That I won't keep doing this
ᵔg things that no longer serve me

I get teary eyes
When I tell myself
That I will leave people alone
Who is not for me

Teary
All teary eyes
Because I backtrack
I go against myself

I hurt myself in the process
I can't keep doing this
Teary
I can't keep doing this to myself

> "I go against myself."
> —Poetic Tamara

Write your own affirmation (s):

_____

_____

_____

_____

_____

_____

35 Direction

I'm going in a direction
That evolves separation
Separation from my old beliefs
Separation from certain individuals

This direction that I'm going in
Is the direction that I must take
I must take it alone
For the time being

"Is the direction that I must take"
—Poetic Tamara

"Check in with yourself."

Force

There's a force

That's all around me

A heavy force

A forceful force

Forcing me

To become a different person

A better person

The person who I am meant to become

This force

Is so powerful

I have a sense that I am

To become my true self

"Is so powerful"

—Poetic Tamara

What does a 'better version of myself' mean to you? It's time to reflect. Sit with yourself.

Without

Without a doubt in mind,

I'm on the right path

Without direct help from a being on this planet

I have gained confidence in my abilities

> "I'm on the right path"
> —Poetic Tamara

"Don't go without saying your affirmations daily."

__Silent__

I don't mind being silent

I love to be left alone with my thoughts

Silent!

Quiet my thoughts

My racing thoughts

My overthinking thoughts

Silent!

Sit still

"My racing thoughts"
-Poetic Tamara

Note down how you are feeling in the present moment:

_____

_____

_____

_____

_____

_____

She loved herself enough to leave

39

She loved herself enough to leave
She chose her
She took awhile
For her to come

To this point in her life
To put herself first
"Better late than never."
Does that phrase fit here?

She loved herself enough to leave
Peace is what she's seeking
Healing is what she's going through
Self-worth, self-value

She loved herself enough to leave
Self-respect is what she's gaining
Self-confidence is what it took
For her to gain courage

was she weak for staying?
Did she become strong when she left?
She's going to have a better life
She loved herself enough to leave

"Healing is what she's going through"

—Poetic Tamara

et something to write on (in) and something to write with.

Now write your own poem.

1-2-3.

Go

Go on

Go on somewhere

I'm getting you out of my system

Leave me be

Exit quickly

40

Why are you here

Not adding value to my life?

Go on

Disappear

Out of my life

Go on

Stopping you

Is not an option of mine

"Exit quickly"

—Poetic Tamara

Write your own affirmation (s):

_____

_____

_____

_____

_____

Done missing you

I used to like you a lot
I think I was falling in love with you
Maybe I was in lust with you
I used to always miss you

Like crazy I did
Hear me out
I'm so
Done missing you

I started to feel like
You weren't really into me
Done missing you
My focus has been shifted

> "You weren't really into me"
> —Poetic Tamara

Jote down how you are feeling in the present moment:

_____

_____

_____

_____

_____

Hold that thought

Wait!

Come again

What nonsense are you talking about?

Hold that thought

I'm not on what you're on

Missed me with that

Hold that thought

I don't want to hear what you have to say

Hold that thought

Re-visit your thought

Before you speak,

Do you even make sense to yourself?

"Re-visit your thought"
—Poetic Tamara

Write your own affirmation (s):

Be patient with yourself

Stop!

Slow down

Wait a bit

Now is the time

Well, the other day

Was the time

For you to focus on you

For you to be patient with yourself

There's no need

To be frustrated

Especially not with yourself

It's important to be patient with yourself

Self-acceptance

Mindfulness

You don't always have to have things figured out

Have patience with yourself

"Slow down"
—Poetic Tamara

"Love yourself. Love yourself. Love yourself."

What are we doing?

44

No dates

We hardly bond with each other

No introductions to family members

So, what are we doing?

Barely communicating effectively with each other

Like really,

What are we doing?

Something has to give

> "We hardly bond with each other"
> —**Poetic Tamara**

Get something to write on (in) and something to write with

Now write your own poem.

1-2-3

Go

45 Sinking quick

I had a day when I didn't
want to get out the bed
That was a kind of day
That I never experienced before

I felt like I was sinking
I was sinking quick
That day shouldn't ever repeat itself
Sinking back

Back into depression
Sinking quick
There was no motivation
I gave in to the negative thoughts

"I felt like I was sinking"
—Poetic Tamara

Write your own affirmation (s):

Only one who loves me

46

I had come to the realization
Again
That nobody loves me
I realized

Again
That I am the only one who loves me
I can tell
Nobody appreciates me

My efforts go unnoticed
I am the only one who loves me
I am the only one who shows me my worth
I feel like I failed myself recently

All because I felt like
I am the only one who loves me
I have to get back right
I have to fill my thoughts and my heart with positivity

> "I am the only one who shows me my worth"
> —Poetic Tamara

47
Individual

I'm the type of individual
Who always lift herself up
I don't call on nobody
I talk to myself

All in my head
This individual
Learned to love
Her alone time

Forced to be an individual
Who is friendless
Who do things on her own
I'm the individual

Who calls on myself
Who calls on God
It's hard doing things on my own
But this individual holds her own weight

"Who do things on her own"

—Poetic Tamara

Jote down how you are feeling in the present moment:

_____

_____

_____

_____

_____

Against yourself

48

Learn from me
I can tell you a lot
About this topic
Listen here

You don't want to
Go against yourself
For by doing so
Will be betraying yourself

Against yourself
Going against yourself
I used to be all in my thoughts
Giving into negative thoughts

This is what will happen
When you go against yourself
You don't want to be at war with yourself
Do you?

"I can tell you a lot"

—Poetic Tamara

"Focus on you."

"Focus on you."

"Focus on you."

Go easy on yourself

49

Give yourself a break

Give yourself a hug

Give yourself a smile

Go easy on yourself

Say your positive affirmations daily

Check in with yourself daily

Sit with yourself daily

Go easy on yourself

"Give yourself a hug"

—Poetic Tamara

~~Don't~~ lift yourself up.

~~Don't~~ inspire yourself.

~~Don't~~ love yourself.

BOOKS BY ANTIONETTE BARNES:

- Poetry From The Heart
- Numb to this single life: A collection of poems for all of the single folks
- Leave me to my thoughts

JOURNAL BY ANTIONETTE BARNES:

- Unlock What's Deep Inside: An Affirmation Journal

www.ingramcontent.com/pod-product-compliance
Lightning Source LLC
Chambersburg PA
CBHW072200070526
44585CB00015B/1234